The Beginner's Guide to Bears

Gillian Shields   Sebastien Braun

ORCHARD BOOKS

You need a bear
And a bear needs you.

You and a bear
Together make two.

What do you look for in a bear?

Soft, gentle, cuddly and warm.

Big...

or small!

Bears like games
In the shining sun,
Though wind and rain
And snow can be fun.

W

hat kind of weather do bears like best?

Sunny days,

rainy days,

snowy days

and windy days.

All kinds
of weather!

Bears love playing,
Bears love toys,
Bears love making
Lots of NOISE!

What toys do bears like best?

Dressing-up clothes . . .

bouncy balls, ducks to push . . .

and pedal cars.
Vroom! Vroom!

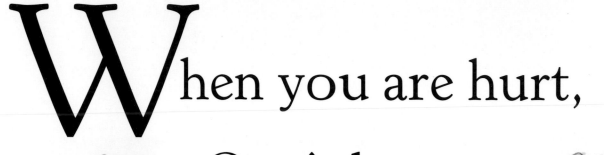

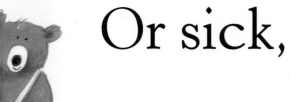 **W**hen you are hurt,

Or sick,

 or sad,

Only your bear

Can make you glad.

What do bears
need when they
don't feel well?

A cuddly pillow . . .

lemonade in bed, a doctor's kit.

Bears love eating
Everything yummy.
Picnics are best for
A bear's hungry tummy.

What do bears love to eat?

Honey, jellybeans, lollipops . . .

ice cream and honey (again).

When it is late
And time for bed,
You cannot sleep
Without your ted.

What do bears need at bedtime?

A cuddly toy and a special blanket.

A glass of milk, night-lights,
a toothbrush and a bedtime story.

Every bear loves
A big bear hug,
Soft and cosy,
Warm and snug.

Who needs a bear?

You need a bear
And a bear needs you.

You and a bear
Together make two.